Explore!
WORLD WAR I

Jane Bingham

LIBRARIES NI
WITHDRAWN FROM STOCK

WAYLAND

First published in 2014 by Wayland

Copyright © Wayland 2014

Wayland
338 Euston Road
London NW1 3BH

Wayland Australia
Level 17/207 Kent Street
Sydney, NSW 2000

 Produced for Wayland by
White-Thomson Publishing
www.wtpub.co.uk
+44 (0)843 208 7460

All rights reserved

Editor: Jane Bingham
Designer: Tim Mayer
Picture researcher: Jane Bingham
Illustrations for step-by-step: Peter Bull
Map illustrator: The Map Studio
Proof reader: Lucy Ross

A cataloguing record for this title is available
from the British Library.

ISBN 978 0 7502 8027 3

Dewey Number 940.3-dc23

10 9 8 7 6 5 4 3 2 1

Printed in Malaysia

Wayland is a division of Hachette Children's
Books, an Hachette UK company

www.hachette.co.uk

Picture acknowledgements:
The author and publisher would like to thank the
following agencies and people for allowing these
pictures to be reproduced:

Cover (top left) Library of Congress; (top right)
Bob Orsillo/Shutterstock; (bottom background)
Wikimedia (bottom left) Ken Backer/Dreamstime;
(bottom right) Skovoroda/Dreamstime; p.1
(left) Eldad Yitzhak/Shutterstock; (right) Susan
Law Cain/ Shutterstock; p.3 Wikimedia; p.4
Wikimedia; p.5 (top) Bob Orsillo/Shutterstock;
(bottom) Library of Congress; p.6 Library
of Congress; p.7 (top) Library of Congress;
(bottom) Deborah Hewitt/Dreamstime; p. 8
Vitezslav Halamka/ Shutterstock; p.9 (top)
Wikimedia; (bottom) Library of Congress; p.11
(top) Library of Congress; (bottom) Wikimedia;
p.12 Nicole Gardner/Dreamstime; p.13 (top)
Susan Law Cain/ Shutterstock; (bottom)
Vitalii Hulai/ Shutterstock; p.14 Skovoroda/
Dreamstime; p.15 (top) Wikimedia; (middle)
Library of Congress; (bottom) Ken Backer/
Dreamstime; p.16 Photowitch/Dreamstime;
p.18 Eldad Yitzhak/Shutterstock; p.19 (top) The
Stapleton Collection/Bridgeman Art Library;
(bottom) Library of Congress; p.20 (top) Susan
Law Cain/ Shutterstock; (bottom) Wikimedia;
p.21 (top) Wikimedia; (bottom) Wikimedia;
p.22 Library of Congress; p.23 (top) Library
of Congress; (bottom) Library of Congress;
p.24 Susan Law Cain/ Shutterstock; p.25 (top)
Library of Congress; (bottom) Christie's Images/
Bridgeman Art Library; p.26 Wikimedia; p.27
(top) Wikimedia; (bottom) Onepony/Dreamstime;
p.28 Nataliia Kasian/Shutterstock; p.29 (top)
Wikimedia; (bottom) Wikimedia.

Please note:
The website addresses (URLs) included in this book were
valid at the time of going to press. However, because of the
nature of the Internet, it is possible that some addresses
may have changed, or sites may have changed or closed
down since publication. While the author and publishers
regret any inconvenience this may cause to the readers,
no responsibility for any such changes can be accepted by
either the author or the publishers.

Contents

What was World War One?

World War One is also known as the First World War and the Great War. It lasted for just four years, from 1914 to 1918, but it involved more countries and killed more people than any other war that had ever been fought before.

Fighting for power

The war began as a struggle for power. At the start of the 20th century there were two rival groups in Europe. Britain, France and Russia were on one side. They were known as the Allies. Germany, Turkey and Austria-Hungary were on the other side. They were known as the Central Powers. The situation between the rivals was very tense, and in 1914 war broke out.

This painting shows the Second Battle of Ypres, fought in Belgium in 1915. An officer is giving orders and soldiers are advancing over enemy land.

Planes were used for spying and for dropping bombs. Pilots had to keep a constant look-out for attacks.

A global war

Much of the fighting took place in northern France and Belgium, in a region called the Western Front. But there were also battles in Russia, Turkey, Italy, the Middle East and Africa. Soldiers from many parts of the world fought for Britain, and in 1917 the USA joined the Allies. As well as the fighting on the ground, there were battles at sea and in the air.

The war to end all wars?

By the end of the war in 1918, over eight million soldiers had died, and another 21 million had been wounded. Many people believed that there could never be such a terrible conflict again. In fact, it was followed by World War Two just 21 years later.

World War One changed the lives of people far away from the fighting. This poster shows women in Britain making weapons in a factory.

WOMEN ARE WORKING DAY & NIGHT TO WIN THE WAR

Y.W.C.A.

£25,000 IMMEDIATELY NEEDED FOR THE
WOMEN'S WAR TIME FUND
TO PROVIDE REST-ROOMS CANTEENS & HOSTELS
LORD SYDENHAM   YOUNG WOMENS   26 GEORGE STREET
Hon TREASURER   CHRISTIAN ASSOCIATION   HANOVER SQUARE. W

The war begins

On 28 June 1914, Archduke Franz Ferdinand was visiting Serbia in Eastern Europe. He was heir to the throne of Austria-Hungary, which had a large and powerful empire in Europe. As Franz Ferdinand was driven through the city of Sarajevo, he was shot dead by a young Serbian rebel. This was the fatal action that started World War One.

Declaring war

One month after Franz Ferdinand's death, Austria-Hungary declared war on Serbia. Germany supported Austria-Hungary, but Serbia had some powerful friends. Russia backed the Serbs, and France supported Russia. Meanwhile, Britain had promised to defend Belgium. When the Germans marched into Belgium, Britain joined the war on the side of Russia and France.

This photograph shows Archduke Franz Ferdinand with his children. As heir to the Empire of Austria-Hungary, he was one of the most powerful men in Europe.

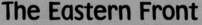

ARE YOU ONE OF KITCHENER'S OWN?

Fighting in France

In the first few weeks of World War One, German soldiers moved fast into northern France, but they were soon stopped by the Allies. The two sides faced each other along a line that became known as the Western Front. By the end of the war, the Western Front stretched through Belgium and eastern France for roughly 645 kilometres (400 miles).

When war was declared, the British Army had only 120,000 men. Posters were put up everywhere urging men to fight for their country. The posters showed Lord Kitchener, the Secretary for War, pointing straight ahead.

The Eastern Front

While the war was raging on the Western Front, the Central Powers were also fighting the Serbs and the Russians. They fought in Eastern Europe in a region that became known as the Eastern Front. During the winter months, troops on the Eastern Front fought in deep snow and suffered terribly from the cold.

This carving shows soldiers marching to war. When the fighting began in summer 1914 most people believed that it would all be over by Christmas.

A terrible struggle

By the end of 1914, there was stalemate on the Western Front. Both sides had built deep trenches and were prepared for a long struggle. The trenches were separated by a strip of ruined land called 'no man's land'.

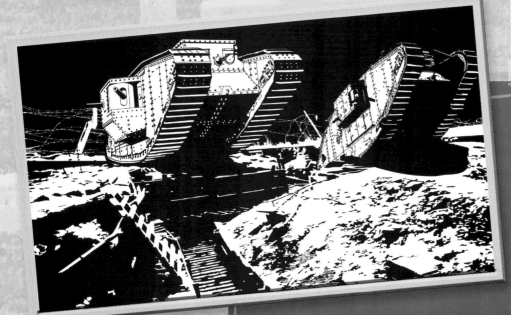

Tanks were used for the first time at the Battle of the Somme. They proved to be deadly killing machines.

On the Western Front

Most of the time, soldiers on both sides made small raids into no man's land, but some major battles were fought on the Western Front. Thousands of men died at Verdun and Passchendaele. Worst of all was the Battle of the Somme, which lasted from July to November 1916. When the fighting ended, the Allies had gained just 10 km (six miles) of land, but over a million soldiers had died.

War at sea

The British and Germans fought each other at the Battle of Jutland, in the North Sea. In just two days in the summer of 1916, 14 British and 11 German ships were sunk. After that, neither side risked their battleships again. Instead, they relied on submarines to launch attacks at sea.

This photograph shows a damaged German battleship after the Battle of Jutland.

The end of the war

In 1917, the USA joined the Allies on the Western Front, and the Allied troops began to advance against the Germans. Meanwhile, the Russians were exhausted, and in March 1918 they made peace with the Central Powers. The Germans made one final push to gain Paris, but they were driven back by the Allies. On 11 November 1918, Germany surrendered and World War One came to an end.

The USA entered the war in April 1917. Posters urged Americans to join the armed forces and play their part in the fighting.

JOIN THE AIR SERVICE and SERVE in FRANCE

DO IT NOW

A worldwide war

World War One was fought in many parts of the world. This was because the countries involved in the conflict had large overseas empires to defend. Germany had colonies in Africa, China and the Pacific, and Turkey controlled most of the Middle East. During the course of the war, Allied troops launched attacks in all these regions.

Overseas troops

Troops arrived from distant parts of the globe to fight in World War One. In particular, many volunteers came from British Commonwealth countries and from the colonies of the British Empire. Canada, Australia, New Zealand, South Africa and India all sent troops to support Britain and fight on the side of the Allies.

Central Powers 1914
Neutral countries later supporting Central Powers
Allies 1914
Neutral countries later supporting Allies
Countries that changed sides from Central Powers to Allies
Countries remaining neutral

EUROPE IN 1914

NORWAY
SWEDEN
FINLAND
DENMARK
RUSSIAN EMPIRE
GREAT BRITAIN
NETHERLANDS
GERMANY
BELGIUM
LUXEMBOURG
POLAND
SWITZERLAND
FRANCE
AUSTRIA-HUNGARY
ROMANIA
BOSNIA
SERBIA
MONTENEGRO
BULGARIA
PORTUGAL
SPAIN
Corsica
ITALY
ALBANIA
Sardinia
GREECE
OTTOMAN EMPIRE (TURKEY)
Sicily
Cyprus

0   500 miles
0   500 kilometres

This map shows the two groups of countries that fought in World War One. At the start of the war, some countries declared that they were neutral and would not fight. Later, they joined in the fighting.

War in the Middle East

In the Middle East, Turkey controlled a vast region called Mesopotamia (covering present-day Iraq, Palestine and Syria). British and Indian troops launched many attacks on Mesopotamia, and they finally captured Baghdad, Palestine and Damascus. In the Arabian Desert, Arab leaders rose up in revolt against the Turks. They were supported by a British army officer called T. E. Lawrence, who became known as Lawrence of Arabia.

World War One had a tragic impact on many parts of the world. This poster was produced in 1918. It appeals for money to help the innocent people whose lives had been ruined by the conflict.

Anzacs at Gallipoli

Troops from Australia and New Zealand were known as Anzacs. They fought bravely on the Western Front and in Turkey. The Anzacs took part in a campaign to land Allied troops in Gallipoli, on the Turkish coast. The landings were a success, but the troops were trapped on the beaches as the Turks resisted any advances. After 10 exhausting months the Allies withdrew. Nothing had been gained and thousands had died.

Anzac soldiers launch an attack at Gallipoli in Turkey.

A soldier's day

Soldiers in the trenches on the Western Front were in constant danger, even when they were not fighting battles. They also suffered terrible living conditions. This imaginary entry from a soldier's dairy describes a typical day on the Western Front.

The day begins before sunrise, when our unit is put on alert. The enemy often attacks at dawn so we need to have our guns at the ready. We hear gunfire and a few explosions, but this time we are lucky.

Most of our work is done at night, so we try to catch up on our sleep during the day. I curl up in a dugout at the back of the trench, but it's very hard to sleep. The lice inside my clothes make me itch horribly and there are rats scrabbling all around me.

The food wagon arrives around 11am. There is watery stew and bread as usual, but it's our only proper meal of the day so we make the most of it. In the afternoon, we boil up some tea. For once it isn't raining so we try to dry out our socks and boots, but they never get really dry.

At sunset we stand by for another enemy attack. Then it is time to join a night patrol into no man's land. My job is to collect any wounded men I can find. Out in no man's land, we are always in danger from enemy gunfire and unexploded shells. Some of us will probably not return to our trench. But we all know that we must do our duty.

The diary entry on this page has been written for this book. Can you create your own diary entry for an imaginary soldier, fighter pilot or nurse? Use the facts in this book and in other sources to help you write about a day in their life.

New technology

At the start of World War One, some men fought like soldiers had done in the past. They rode horses into battle and were armed with swords. But this way of fighting could not last. By 1916, armies were using tanks to stand up to machine gun attacks. Other new technology included barbed wire, gas masks, telephones and radios.

Guns and tanks

Some machine guns used in World War One could fire up to 600 bullets a minute. Soldiers were powerless against this hail of bullets, so tanks were developed to protect them. Tanks could advance over muddy ground, flattening barbed wire and providing a shield for an advancing army.

Tanks were made from thick steel sheets, riveted together. Their wide caterpillar tracks allowed them to move over uneven ground without tipping over.

Poison gas and masks

During the Battle of Ypres in 1915, French troops were surrounded by a cloud of greenish-yellow gas. In minutes, they were choking and falling to the ground, gasping for breath. Soon, armies on both sides were making use of this deadly weapon. Some used chlorine gas that caused choking. Some used mustard gas that caused blisters and burns and could lead to blindness. By 1917, gas masks had been designed that could protect soldiers from poison gas, but not before thousands had died in agony.

This is a German field telephone with a battery box.

Gas masks covered the entire head and had a tube leading to an air tank.

Telephones and radios

Telephones were the main method of communication in World War One. Cables were dug between the trenches and the generals' headquarters, and field telephones were set up. Messages could also be sent by radio. Pilots in observation planes sent radio messages to operators on the ground.

Send a message in Morse code

Radio operators in World War One sent their messages in Morse code. Radio signals were weak, so it was hard to hear a human voice. Morse code messages could be heard much more easily than human voices because they were made up of clear, loud sounds.

Messages were sent using a simple Morse code transmitter. The operator pressed on the black button to produce a loud buzzing sound.

What is Morse code?

Morse code letters are made up of short and long sounds. These sounds can be made by a radio buzzer or by a whistle. To make a short sound, the buzzer is held down for just a second. To make a long sound, it is held down for three seconds.

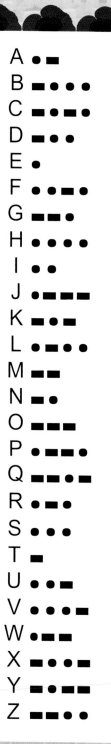

A	·▬
B	▬···
C	▬·▬·
D	▬··
E	·
F	··▬·
G	▬▬·
H	····
I	··
J	·▬▬▬
K	▬·▬
L	·▬··
M	▬▬
N	▬·
O	▬▬▬
P	·▬▬·
Q	▬▬·▬
R	·▬·
S	···
T	▬
U	··▬
V	···▬
W	·▬▬
X	▬··▬
Y	▬·▬▬
Z	▬▬··

The Morse code alphabet

When the Morse code alphabet is written down, the sounds are shown by dots and dashes. A short sound is a dot. A long sound is a dash.

Send and receive a message

You can send and receive your own Morse code messages. Instead of using a radio buzzer to send your signals, simply whistle the short and long sounds! A short sound should last for one second. A long sound should last for three seconds. Leave a 5-second gap between each letter and a 10-second gap between each word.

Write out your message in Morse code (using dots and dashes) before you send it. Then whistle your message. Your friends can use dots and dashes to note down the letters they hear. Then they can work out what your message says.

SOS!

The most famous Morse code message is SOS. It is very easy to remember: three dots, then three dashes, then three dots again. People all over the world recognize it as an emergency signal.

Planes, airships and submarines

W orld War One was not only fought on the ground. Planes, airships, ships and submarines all had an important part to play in the fighting.

Planes

The first warplanes were used for observation. Pilots flew small, light planes over enemy lines and reported on what they saw. By the end of the war, heavier aircraft had been developed. They were used to bomb enemy targets. Pilots were in danger from anti-aircraft guns on the ground and from enemy planes in the air. They fought daring battles in the sky, known as dogfights.

In 1914, planes were still a very new invention. The first flight had taken place just 11 years earlier!

Airships

Airships were filled with hydrogen gas to make them lighter than air. In the early years of the war, they were used for bombing raids, but by 1916 incendiary bullets had been invented. These bullets could set fire to hydrogen gas and destroy an airship in minutes. After 1916, airships were used only for observation at sea.

This painting shows a German airship lit up by searchlights. Powerful anti-aircraft guns on the ground shot at airships and planes.

Submarines

Submarines played a key part in the war. They travelled silently under the ocean and launched torpedoes (underwater bombs) at enemy ships. The German submarines, known as U-boats, were extremely successful in their attacks. Between 1914 and 1918, 274 U-boats sank 6,596 ships.

In this scene, a German U-boat is surfacing after it has torpedoed an enemy ship.

Women at war

These women are members of the Salvation Army. They are making doughnuts for soldiers at the front.

Women played an active part in World War One. Some had jobs close to the battle front. Many more worked in their home country. When the men went off to fight in the war, women often took over their jobs. They helped to keep their country running until the men returned.

Women at the front

Some women worked as nurses in army field hospitals. Others were bakers and cooks, providing food for the soldiers. Many French women set up laundries to wash clothes and blankets for the Allied forces.

This American poster shows a Red Cross nurse.

Work at home

On the home front, women took on a range of jobs. Some worked in hospitals for recovering soldiers. Some were employed by the army and supported the troops by organizing supplies and communications. Others worked in factories, on railways and in dockyards, taking the place of the men who had gone off to fight. In Britain, thousands of women joined the Women's Land Army, and helped to produce food for the troops.

This painting shows women working in the fields to help the war effort. It was painted in 1917.

Women in danger

Some brave women risked their lives in the war. Edith Cavell ran a nursing school in Brussels, Belgium. When the city was occupied by German troops, she decided to stay and shelter 200 British soldiers. Mata Hari was a famous dancer who worked as a spy for the French Secret Service. Sadly, both women were arrested and killed by the Germans.

Mata Hari danced in cities all over Europe, and met men in very high positions. This made her a perfect spy for the Allies.

On the home front

I n their home countries, people faced many changes to their old way of life. Most families had close relatives who were far away, fighting for their country. People were desperate for letters, but they dreaded hearing bad news.

Your Work means Victory

Build another One

UNITED STATES SHIPPING BOARD   EMERGENCY FLEET CORPORATION

Posters encouraged people at home to play their part in the war by helping to build ships, tanks and weapons.

War factories

As soon as the war started, governments began to take over factories. They used these factories to make weapons, ammunition and vehicles for their armed forces. Most of the factory workers were women.

Workers in munitions factories produced bullets and other explosives. They worked with a range of chemicals, including sulphur, which turned their skin and hair yellow. It was later discovered that these chemicals had a very bad effect on the workers' health.

These women are making bullets in a munitions factory.

Food shortages

Large amounts of food were needed for the troops, so it was in short supply at home. The British government urged people not to waste food. They also encouraged families to keep chickens and grow their own fruit and vegetables. The German people suffered especially badly because the Allies managed to stop most food supplies from reaching Germany.

Bombing raids

People lived in fear of bombing raids. During the course of the war, the German air force carried out over 100 raids on Britain. These caused much less damage than the bombs of World War Two, but they were still very frightening. In 1915, German airships made 20 bombing raids, killing 181 people, and injuring another 455 victims.

Was England will!

People all over Europe were terrified of bombing raids. This frightening German poster shows an imagined attack from the air.

Picturing the war

How do we know about World War One? Many people wrote letters and kept diaries. Some soldiers wrote poems or memoirs about their time at the front. Artists and photographers recorded the horrors of battle and the details of the soldiers' daily lives. All these sources help us to imagine the experience of war. They have also inspired some modern authors to write about the war.

Poems

Some great poets served as soldiers in World War One. One of the best-known war poets is Wilfred Owen. He wrote about the sufferings of the soldiers on the Western Front. He also asked some difficult questions. What was the point of the war and why did so many young men have to die?

Photographers captured the reality of life in the trenches.

Paintings

Artists were sent to the battle fronts to record the war. The British artist Stanley Spencer painted ambulance workers carrying wounded soldiers on stretchers. Another British artist, Paul Nash, showed the ruined landscape of the Western Front, with blackened stumps of trees and seas of mud.

Stories

The children's author Michael Morpurgo has written several novels about World War One. His most famous story is *War Horse*. It describes the horrific experiences of a farm-horse called Joey, who was sent to the Western Front. *War Horse* has been made into a play and a film.

The American artist John Singer Sargent painted this moving scene. His painting is called *Gassed*. It shows a line of men who have all been blinded by mustard gas.

After the War

In November 1918, Germany surrendered and the war ended. People everywhere were relieved that the fighting was over, but life was still very hard. The countries that had fought in the war took a long time to recover. There was widespread unemployment and it was especially difficult for wounded men to find work.

The Treaty of Versailles was signed in the Hall of Mirrors at the Palace of Versailles in France.

A dangerous treaty

In 1919, the Allies and Germany met in France and agreed to sign the Treaty of Versailles. The treaty demanded that Germany should pay enormous sums of money to the Allies. This led to great suffering, and many German people resented the Allies. In the 1930s, Adolf Hitler encouraged these feelings of resentment and gained widespread support for his war against France and Britain. Historians believe that the Treaty of Versailles helped to cause the outbreak of World War Two.

British women had been campaigning for the right to vote since the 1860s. They finally made some progress in 1918.

Women's rights

World War One helped to create some major changes in society. While the men were away, many women grew used to working outside the home, and when the war was over, they wanted this freedom to continue. Change did not happen rapidly, but gradually women began to play a more active role in society. The changing status of women was recognised in 1918, when the British government granted the right to vote to women over the age of 30.

Remembering the war

After the war, governments in many parts of the world decided to hold special services of remembrance for all the people who had died. Services were held on 11 November, the anniversary of the day that World War One ended. Today, Remembrance Services are still held all over the world on 11 November.

On Remembrance Day, wreaths are laid on war memorials in memory of the dead. This memorial is in Canada.

Facts and figures

The human cost

• More than 65 million men from 30 countries fought in World War One.

• Over 8 million died.

• Around 21 million were wounded.

• The Allies lost about 5 million soldiers.

• The Central Powers lost about 3 million soldiers.

Tyne Cot Cemetery in Belgium has almost 12,000 graves. The graves belong to soldiers from the British Commonwealth who fought in World War One.

On the Western Front

• The line of trenches on the Western Front stretched for roughly 645 km (400 miles).

• Explosives used at the Battle of Ypres in Belgium could be heard in London 220 km (140 miles) away.

• The Germans were the first to use flamethrowers in World War One. They could fire jets of flame as far as 40 m (130 ft).

The first tank made in World War One was given the nickname 'Little Willie'. It had a top speed of 4.8 km per hour (3 miles per hour).

Animals in war

One of the many dangers that horses faced was poison gas. In this photograph, a soldier is fitting a gas mask onto a horse.

• More than 500,000 pigeons carried messages between headquarters and the front lines.

• Some pigeons had a camera strapped to their chest. It was designed to take pictures of the enemy.

• Red Cross dogs were trained to go in search of wounded soldiers. They carried a First Aid kit around their necks.

• Some soldiers kept stray cats as pets. The cats helped to kill the rats that lived in the trenches.

• By 1917, Britain had over a million horses and mules working for the armed forces.

• Over the course of the war, Britain lost over 484,000 horses – one horse for every two men.

All figures on these pages are approximate.

Glossary

Allies The group of countries that fought with Britain in World War One.

ammunition Bullets, bombs and other explosive weapons.

anniversary A date that people remember because something important happened then.

British Commonwealth A group of countries that used to be ruled by Britain.

Central Powers The group of countries that fought with Germany in World War One.

colonies Countries that have been settled in by people from another country, and are controlled by that country.

communications Ways of making contact and staying in touch.

dugout A small space that has been dug out of the earth.

empire A group of countries that all have the same ruler.

hand-grenade A small bomb that is thrown by hand.

heir Someone who has the right to another person's title, property or money when that person dies.

hydrogen A gas that is lighter than air and that catches fire easily.

memoir A piece of writing that tells the story of part of the writer's life.

merchant ships Ships that carry cargo, such as food.

no man's land An area between two enemy forces that has not been captured by either side.

observation The act of watching something carefully.

occupied Taken over by an enemy.

rebel Someone who protests or fights against something.

Red Cross An international organisation that provides medical help in wars and other disasters.

resent To feel hurt and angry.

Salvation Army A Christian organisation that provides help and support for people in need.

source Something that provides information.

stalemate A situation where nobody can make a move.

surrender To give up in a fight and admit that you are beaten.

torpedo An underwater missile that explodes when it hits anything.

typical Something that has the characteristics and qualities of a particular type of person or thing.

unemployment Lack of jobs.

unit A small group of soldiers.

Western Front A large area of land in northern France and Belgium where much of the fighting took place in World War One.

Further reading

War in the Trenches: Remembering World War One, Peter Hicks (Wayland, 2013)
World War I (Machines that Won the War), Charlie Samuels (Wayland, 2013)
World War One (True Stories), Clive Gifford (Wayland, 2013)
The Trenches: A First World War Soldier, 1914-1918 (My Story), Jim Eldridge (Scholastic, 2008)
World War I (Eye-Witness Guides), Simon Adams (Dorling Kindersley, Re-issue edition, 2011)

Websites

http://www.bbc.co.uk/history/worldwars/wwone/
A BBC website written by subject experts. It includes a virtual tour of life in the trenches.

http://www.bbc.co.uk/schools/worldwarone/
A BBC website designed for children. It has a section on True Lives with diaries, letters, scrapbooks, newspaper cuttings, photos and keepsakes, and an interactive battle strategy game.

http://www.firstworldwar.com/index.htm
A multi-media history of World War One, including audio and video clips, photographs and posters.

Index

Africa 5, 10
airships 18, 19
Allies 4, 5, 7, 8, 9, 10, 11, 21, 23, 26, 28, 30
ambulances 20, 25
ammunition 22, 30
Anzacs 17
armed forces 9, 22, 29
Austria-Hungary 4, 6

barbed wire 14
battles 4, 8, 9, 15, 29
battleships 9
Belgium 4, 5, 6, 7, 21, 28, 29, 30
bombs 5, 18, 19, 23, 30
Britain 4, 5, 6, 10, 21, 23, 126, 29, 30
British Commonwealth 10, 28, 30
bullets 13, 14, 19, 22, 23, 30

Cavell, Edith 21
Central Powers 4, 7, 9, 28, 30
colonies 10, 30

diaries 12, 13, 24, 31
dugouts 12, 30

Eastern Front 7
empires 6, 10, 30
enemies 4, 5, 12, 13, 18, 19, 29, 30

factories 5, 21, 22, 23
flamethrowers 29
France 4, 5, 6, 7, 26, 30
Franz Ferdinand, Archduke 6

French Secret Service 21

gas masks 15, 29
gasses 14, 15, 19, 25, 30
Germany 4, 6, 9, 10, 23, 26, 30
governments 22, 23, 27
Great War 4
guns 14, 18, 19

Hari, Mata 21
Hitler, Adolf 26
horses 14, 25, 29
hospitals 20

Italy 5

Kitchener, Lord 7

Lawrence, T.E. 11
London 29

memoirs 24, 30
Middle East 5, 10, 11
Morpurgo, Michael 25
Morse code 16, 17

Nash, Paul 25
no man's land 8, 13, 30
nurses 13, 20, 21

Owen, Wilfred 24

peace 9, 26
pilots 5, 13, 15, 18
planes 5, 15, 18, 19

radios 14, 15, 16, 17
raids 8, 19, 23
rats 12, 29
Red Cross 20, 29, 30
Remembrance Day 27
Russia 4, 5, 6

Salvation Army 20, 30
Serbia 6
Sargent, John Singer 25
soldiers 4, 5, 7, 8, 11, 12, 13, 14, 15, 20, 21, 24, 25, 26, 28, 29, 30, 31
Spencer, Stanley 25
submarines 9, 18, 19

tanks 8, 14, 15, 22, 29
telephones 14, 15
torpedoes 19, 30
trenches 8, 12, 13, 15, 24, 29, 31
Turkey 4, 5, 10, 11

U-boats 19
unemployment 26, 30
USA 5, 19

Versailles, Treaty 26

weapons 5, 15, 22, 30
Western Front 5, 7, 8, 9, 11, 12, 24, 25, 29, 30
Women's Auxiliary Army 21
Women's Land Army 21
World War Two 5, 23, 26

Explore!

Who were the Victorians?
Queen Victoria's reign
Empire and exploration
Rich and poor
Working life
Health and medicine
A Victorian schoolchild's diary
Scientists and inventors
Engineers and builders
All kinds of transport
Artists, writers and photographers
Make a thaumatrope
Facts and figures

978 0 7502 8037 2

Who were the Romans?
The rise of Rome
A mighty power
The Roman world
Town and country
Family and school
Religion and worship
A Roman child's day
Entertainment and leisure
Building technology
Artists and writers
Make a mosaic
Facts and figures

978 0 7502 8098 3

What was World War One?
The war begins
A terrible struggle
A worldwide war
A soldier's day
New technology
Send a message in Morse code
Planes, airships and submarines
Women at war
On the home front
Picturing the war
After the war
Facts and figures

978 0 7502 8027 3

Who were the Ancient Egyptians?
Early kingdoms
A mighty power
The Egyptian world
Religion and beliefs
Everyday life
A day at a temple school
Feasting and fun
Brilliant buildings
Medicine, science and magic
Art, music and writing
Write in hieroglyphics
Facts and figures

978 0 7502 8097 6

What was World War Two?
The war begins
A worldwide war
The final stages
The holocaust
On the home front
Keeping safe
A letter from wartime London
Science in war
Send a coded message
Technology in war
Picturing the war
Facts and figures

978 0 7502 8038 9

Who were the Ancient Greeks?
Early Greeks
A great civilization
The Greek world
Family life
Gods and goddesses
Games and plays
A day at the Olympic Games
Make a theatrical mask
Maths, science and medicine
Architects and builders
Art and ideas
Facts and figures

978 0 7502 8099 0

Who were the Tudors?
Two powerful kings
Edward, Mary, Elizabeth
Rich and poor
A kitchen-maid's day
Making Tudor gingerbread
Tudor towns
Tudor entertainments
Exploring the world
Traders and settlers
Science and technology
Artists, musicians and writers
Facts and figures

978 0 7502 8036 5

Who was William Shakespeare?
Young William
A great success
All sorts of plays
Shakespeare's England
The wider world
Shakespeare's London
The Globe Theatre
Make a model theatre
Actors and playwrights
A boy actor's day
Music and art
Facts and figures

978 0 7502 8135 5